A Maker's Guide

A Maker's Guide

Amy Howard

Founder and CEO of Amy Howard at Home®

Editor: Tarra Kruzan
Layout & Design: Candace Joseph
Photography: Annabella Charles, except for page 10, 104
(left and bottom) and 107 by Allison Rodgers, and page
174 by Ashleigh Peak

ISBN: 978-0-692-47180-7

Printed by Progress Printing Plus in Virginia, U.S.A.

FSC® is a non-profit international organization established to promote
the responsible management of the world's forests. Products carrying
the FSC label are independently certified to assure consumers that
they come from forests that are managed to meet the social, economic
and ecological needs of present and future generations, and other
controlled sources.

Find out more about Progress Printing Plus and the environment at
progressprintplus.com/services/sustainability

Contents

Foreword

by Debbi Fields of Mrs.Fields

We all have a heartbeat – we know it well. We find our rhythms in the steady days, the unpredictable adventures and those impassable hurdles that steal our breath. To know your beat is to march along, no matter the terrain. To know Amy's beat, is to catch a glimpse of an electrical pulse that will set your life ablaze.

The first time I met Amy, I recognized something very different was embedded inside of her. I was in a new season of my entrepreneurial journey at Mrs. Fields Cookies and found that her passion and fervency inspired me in my own walk. I hadn't just found a new friend, I found someone who could see right into what made me individual.

Over the years I have watched Amy's business grow. Her innovative ideas, phenomenal taste and pure joy for life sets her apart. It would be easy to take such accomplishments and hold them up for the world to see, but that's not her. The generosity of Amy's open heart is displayed in her uncanny ability to dive into what makes each of us who we are – our dreams.

When I received word about A Maker's Guide, I knew Amy had done it again. This body of work is much more than a book, it's a necessity. We all need words of affirmation – someone to tell us that who we are and what we do matters. These words will bring rebirth to your dreams. Revisit them often and believe: This life is not just about living, it's about following your hearts.

Love and kisses,
Debbi

Navigating this Book

When you open a page filled with a **single enlarged sentence**, read it as something I want you to never forget. Take each word to heart and ponder it. The words you find emboldened and standing alone have been carefully chosen to give you encouragement and insight. We all need mementos; these are yours.

The **words of wisdom** you will see located at the top corner of the pages are filled with a wealth of appended information. View these insights as necessary tools you can readily reference throughout your journey. I want to fill your mind with as much useful information as I can offer. These wise words are what I myself have put into practice during my own journey. I believe it is important to have small digestible nuggets of key of information as you travel these uncharted waters.

The outlined boxes on the left sides are what I like to call **challenge centers**. These small but impactful calls to action will provide you with imperative to-do lists. Do not flip to the next chapter until you have completed your challenge. One may ask you to write something out; the other will ask you to examine or shift your habits. Each one will serve as an impetus to the next chapter in your journey. Dreams are just dreams until your actions bring purpose.

Each chapter also includes **interactive questions** to answer. These serve as the tangible application of our conversation. In time, the answers you write will reveal how this book has led you to your prosperity. My hope is that each chapter will strike a resonant chord in your being. Hold tight and never let go.

Introduction

Dear Maker,

You have known since you were very young that you possess individual qualities that make you all your own.

Those qualities speak volume to the people around you and have become the things you are known for. For as long as I can remember, I have loved creating. Now that I am an adult, that creativity has taken on many forms. Some days it can be painting a piece of furniture for our home. Other days, it can be devising a business solution to help my team become more efficient. In the past I have wondered whether my joy resides more in creating art for its own sake or art for its business potential. Over the course of my life as a creative entrepreneur, I have found a balanced truth to share with you, your work and passions can collide.

Uncovering your dreams to reveal the purpose of your gifts will change the course of your life. The mission to use your purpose should always combine two things: something that will solve a problem for other people and something that you naturally already do. No matter who you are, you have passions that you have been chasing after your entire life. Even in the smallest measure, you have made these passions a priority. My message to you is that in those talents and desires, somewhere in those passions, lies your business. Take heart dear maker, it might not be the obvious answer.

You would not be picking up this book in the first place if you did not have an internal spark of an entrepreneurial spirit. If your goal, as a creative, is to develop your deep-rooted passion in such a way that you are able to focus on it full time, you are going to have to monetize it. In order to be financially successful, your passions and business ventures have to become one. When you dedicate your energy and align your choices to a path that feeds into your dream, you can accomplish extraordinary feats. The freedom to make a living doing what you love is the key to a full life of unending adventure.

Historically, art has supplied society with insight as to how the culture is evolving. However, as an artist, you don't always know how to bring others into your world view let alone make a living doing so. As you read this book, I want it to be as though we were friends meeting for coffee. I will share with you my successes and failures, as well as a road map that leads you to a fully functioning business using your creative passions. I want to encourage you that no matter who you are or where you are, your dreams and giftings have a place. Simply wishing and waiting won't get you anywhere. Your dreams require hard work and sacrifice. This journey is not about compromise, but rather moving forward so you do not look back with regrets. Ask yourself one very important question: What am I willing to pursue like my life depends on it? Because, dear maker, it does.

The DNA
of Your
Dreams

Dreaming

As children, we dream out loud. There was a time in your life when you knew you could be anything you wanted.

Dress up was a means of expression and plans to be president didn't seem implausible. Looking at the world through your brand new set of eyes, you could clearly see the endless possibilities ahead. In time, however, constraint took hold and in the face of adulthood your childlike faith grew dull. Believing that you could be a superhero who flies or a ballerina who dances her way around the world, proved hollow.

DREAMING OUT LOUD

Real life is often assumed to be the laying down of our childlike dreams to make room for grown-up responsibilities. For most of you, this meant settling into a respectable career you don't love. Reality doesn't have to be that scary. Hiding your dreams beneath layers of obligation has never suited anyone and it never will. The need to dream never disappears. In fact, as you grow older and more aware of this world, dreams become more and more vital to your well-being.

When you work at a job you hate, you dread the work week. Some days, simply driving there induces anxiety. Counting down the hours until the torture will end cannot be the way you envisioned living your life. The greatest tragedy of this depressive state is that you are dying a slow death from within and don't even realize it. You have replaced the value of purpose with a life of survival.

Dear maker, somewhere along the way, you lost hope in your dreams and you compromised. I would never minimize how, at the time, you felt you had no other choice. No one ever says they want to settle. None of us would ever plan to live imprisoned by unhappiness, but that's where a majority of you are. You couldn't afford the tuition to your dream college. You didn't see any other open doors. You knew your children needed provisions, so you gave in and took that job. It was too risky to keep up the pursuit of a dying dream and you laid it aside.

Life is a journey.

We have all experienced the elation of victory and the blight of loss along the road. For some however, those failures and the fear of our shortcomings weighed heavy. So heavy, in fact, that they lost their confidence to dream. The pursuit of authenticity as an adult can be painstaking. We look to those who appear to have it all together for clues to the direction of happiness. Each one of us craves assurance we are choosing the right path. Living in someone else's likeness will never be your right path. You know yours, it's found in your deepest desires.

CONSIDER THIS As an adult, saying your dream out loud can be one of the most intimidating steps you can ever take. Before you turn the page, I want you to write down your dream; in detail. No matter how big or how unbelievable it may seem, you need to put it into writing. I recommend displaying these precious words somewhere you will pass by everyday. Before you know it, your dream won't seem as far-fetched as before.

Believing in the significance of your dream is the simple act of admitting it is a part of you that will never go away. I encourage you to share your dream with a close confidant. Nothing that is hidden can grow in effectiveness. When you admit your dream out loud, it is birthed. Ask your friend to become your accountability partner during your journey. More than anything, your success demands you never lose heart.

I WANT YOU TO CLOSE YOUR EYES AND REMEMBER WHERE YOU WERE YOUR HAPPIEST AS A CHILD.

What were you doing?

Where were you?

THINK OF YOUR ADOLESCENCE

Where were you in your happiest, most fulfilled memories?

What were you doing?

THINK ABOUT TODAY.

As an adult, what are you doing when you are your happiest?

What work fulfills you more than anything else nowadays?

You were born with everything you need to be you. There is still time to dream.

You have been busy, dear maker. For some, making a living, providing for your family and the pursuit of comfort has had you distracted for so long, you forgot how to dream. If your dream is dead, it's time to get a new dream. The revelries you carried as a child and those that still, to this day, fulfill you deeper than anything else, that is where your dreams will always derive.

GOING BACK TO YOUR FIRST LOVE

Everyone wants to feel important. You were made with hope inside of you. Hope that you would have a place in this world and that who you are, just as you came, has value and purpose. You have hidden that hope for far too long now. I implore you to rethink the value of comfort compared to the value of living in the freedom of your dreams. The first change you have to make is to realize this: it's not too late. The worth you saw in yourself, long ago in your childhood, still and always will have a rightful place in this world. You were born with everything you need to be you. There is still time to dream.

Gifting + Passion = Purpose

Not everyone would say they want to make a living out of their dream. But everyone does want to do what they love, all the time. Isn't that a dream?

Who wouldn't want to use their strengths and talents for a greater purpose in life? When your gifts and passions work in tandem, they shed light on your purpose. Many people think they could never quit their job and live on what they would earn on their own. Dear maker, once you begin to chase after your dream, you will have so much more potential to see it through and become successful.

Mediocrity is a choice, just as it is a choice to follow your dreams. When you live your life pouring yourself into your passion, every opportunity feels like a privilege. Living a privileged life is based on one singular truth: A life of privilege is a life granted its source of pleasure.

Embracing your talents is accepting the gift of opportunity. When you understand and welcome the gifts and passions that make you individual, you are staring the importance of your purpose right in the face. Taking this opportunity to heart requires courage, but remember: playing it safe has never been life giving. Singers want to sing, painters want to paint, and teachers want to teach. The most unnatural path in life is to not do what you were made to do.

In my youth I was told that I would make a terrific lawyer. I even enrolled in a few law classes in college. I soon realized, however, that while the legal field would have been a respectable career, it wasn't my dream. I might have made my fair share of money, but every dollar would have been spent in discontent. It is dangerous to live confined by other people's dreams for you. Good advice has its place, but If you aren't working within your convictions and passions you will never own your work. Life isn't about living up to someone else's expectations and desires, it's about the freedom to be yourself. Living to please others or complete their vision of you is a trap.

I have been a creative loner for most of my life. Making my own way and not having to work for anyone else has always been deeply woven into my aspirations. When I was a stay at home mom with young children, I craved a creative outlet. I would design typography displays for their rooms during their naps, cutting out little wooden animals in the shapes of the alphabet. A was an aardvark; B was a bird; C was little cockatoo and so on. Eventually I rented a booth at the local farmer's market, bringing boxes filled with the letter language I created. I encouraged children to create a display of their own. Seeing the elation in their smiles as they spelled out their names with something I made was life giving. At the time, I thought I was simply earning extra money doing something I loved. I understand now that I was practicing how to pursue the business of my passions.

No matter who you are, you have passions you have been chasing your entire life. Even in the smallest measure, you have made these passions of yours a priority. What wakes you up in the morning? What drives you in your work and personal life? I like to call these my Value Drivers. Mine are excellence, creativity, and harmony. I want to work and live to the best of my ability. Creativity is in everything. It can be painting a chair, decorating my home, or simply dreaming up a business solution. My conviction for harmony shows in every facet of my life. I want everyone around me to know they are valued and I want to know that they are at ease.

Knowing what is important to you will also reveal where you shut down. Perhaps you have been advised to suppress your dream – your big idea. The doodler failing math class was an artist struggling to find his place in the world. The talker in study hall repeatedly sent to detention could inspire others as a prolific speaker. When given the proper outlets, your creative self will blossom and mature. But fear and apprehension will only shield you from the critical outlets you need to mature your gifts. The anxiety and burden you carry from living a lie will make your life miserable. You won't feel free living outside of your desires, you'll feel trapped. Working an hour at something you are not gifted in is harder than working a full day at the tasks you were made to do.

What can I do better than anyone else around me?

What three talents do I like in myself?

If there were no limitations, what work would I do?

MONEY IS A BYPRODUCT OF
PURSUING YOUR PASSIONS,
NEVER THE GOAL. OVER 86%
OF ALL MILLIONAIRES ARE
SELF-MADE ENTREPRENEURS.
WEALTH IS ONLY GAINED
AFTER DEDICATION,
PERSEVERANCE, PLANNING,
SELF-DISCIPLINE AND
FREEDOM BECOME YOUR
MAIN FOCUS.

My message to you, dear maker, is that in those talents and desires – somewhere in those passions – lies your purpose. It might not be the obvious answer. For me, I could have had a successful career as an interior designer, but I craved to be on the other end. I wanted to be the creator of beautiful things, of the luxury furnishings other interior designers would use. What you are passionate about will become the mantra for the business of your dreams.

Success never comes all at once. In this journey, we are all practicing to perfect our crafts. When you hear a concert pianist, you think you could never replicate the magnitude of that excellence. But that art form has been around for centuries. Why? Because the artists are dedicated to the small strides needed to achieve awe-inspiring perfection. When you are enthusiastic about the opportunity to pursue what you love, others will take notice. Passion is contagious. It is not difficult to do what you were made to do. It is as easy as falling off a rock.

Who You Are

Transparency is attractive. It allows you to live and interact authentically with everyone around you. But without understanding and embracing who you are, you can't live transparently.

When you are blind to your own best attributes, you fall into the trap of misunderstanding your own personality. Dear maker, if you are hiding the traits that are specific only to you, you are hiding from your own reality. Everyone has strengths as well as weaknesses. We all have character flaws we wish we could change. Those should be shaped and matured, not hidden.

Living free is understanding that while your weaknesses need to be cultivated, your strengths are the life-line to your integrity.

Too many of us believe that who we are, how we are designed, isn't enough. We believe we must be remodeled to be accepted. In life, there are no right or wrong personality types. How you came is how you are meant to be. Each and every one of us provides an integral part to making this world rich and whole. You have to be you and everyone else has to be themselves. Why be convinced it is easier to suppress, conform, or put on a mask? You were made for specific tasks in life and knowing yourself is vital to recognizing those tasks.

DNA | DISC

The DISC personality assessment is my go-to, reveal-all source for understanding myself, my family, and my staff. The results not only spell out your strengths and weaknesses, but how you can communicate and work best with other personality types. I find it to be life changing for most people. Your personal and business relationships will flourish in light of the invaluable insight the results offer. Take the free 15-minute test online at www.tonyrobbins.com/disc-profile. Those initial results will impart enough information to get you started. Don't be dismayed; this is not a paid advertisement. I believe in the importance of self-realization so fully that I want to share my most valued resources with you. The results will break down into four personality types:

Dominant, Inspiring, Cautious and Supportive.

You will be strong in two or three areas. Your Value Drivers center around four personality styles: Task-oriented, people-oriented, fast paced, and reserved.

After seeing your results, you might be shocked, or perhaps you will find they explain everything you've been questioning. The good news is: there isn't an ideal mold to fill, nor a more valued personality type to possess. When my husband, Gene, and I completed our personality assessment, it was a confirmation of what we already knew. We are complete opposites. I am off the charts in the dominant and inspiring categories. There isn't a person on earth with whom I could not strike up a conversation or a problem for which I don't have an answer. Gene, however, is steady, detail-oriented, and one of the most intellectually oriented human beings I know. He scores very high in supportive and cautious traits. I may be a bold visionary, but Gene is my rock. We could believe the rumors that say we don't fit together or that we should alter who we are to fill the ideal description of a man or woman. While our traits couldn't be more different, our strengths act like body parts playing their role in the operation of our relationship. Together, we make a whole person.

Each and every one of us provides an <u>integral part</u> to making this world rich and whole.

Dear maker, lack of self awareness brings about misery in your work environment as well as conflict in your personal life. Being cognizant of how each personality plays a vital role in every operation will boost your initiative to ensure you and those around you are working within your individual strengths.

For example, if you are a combination of dominant and inspiring on the DISC assessment, you tend to be decisive and quick to get the job done. You are an influencer. Your personality allows you to be the best sale representative for your business. There is no sense in seeking out sales help when you are first getting started. While influencers are very personable, they are rarely detail oriented. Thus a supportive bookkeeper might be your ideal first hire. If you are a combination of dominant and cautious however, you might struggle to relate to new faces. You may need to hire a motivated sales member so you can be free to focus on your budget and investment decisions. No matter what your personality, you will have to get your mission across. When you are working within your passions and strengths, there is always a way.

All personality types are valuable and necessary. Degrading yourself or others because you don't understand each other will destroy the hard work you put into your projects. Knowing how you operate and how others around you thrive can save the relationships, process, and mission behind the business of your purpose. Life is not a game of pretend, dear maker. Becoming self-realized is to understand who you are and love it. Live it out in integrity and move on. Your adventure awaits.

CONSIDER THIS Before you read any further, please take the free 15-minute DISC assessment at www.tonyrobbins.com/disc-profile. Answer the questions with honesty and openness. Never answer as you want to be portrayed. This is a chance to get realistic and encouraging advice based on the real you.

Who you are, is who you were made to be. Look at the positive and the negative of your personality breakdown. Research and read about your personality type and how to bring out the best about it. The next chapters will guide you through setting goals, how to build community and the art of self-discipline. When you are aware of how you ideally operate and in turn thrive, you see where you need to be focusing and relieving yourself. This could be life changing.

What are your personality types?

What are five great features of your personality?

What are five tasks you excel at given your personality strengths?

Which personality areas of yours can be matured and sharpened?

Timing Is Everything

*"Are we there yet? How much longer? Are we there
yet?" Oftentimes our dreamy eyes gaze too far into
the future, without regarding the present.*

Constant pursuit without reflection can, all too soon, morph into
paralyzing defeatism. The opportunities and allowances you had
ten years ago might not be the same as those that you have now,
but you have been growing in skill and maturity. Your priorities and
responsibilities will change throughout your life. Do not wallow in the
notion of bygone opportunities or be frozen by cynicism. Dear maker,
you have to treat every stage in life as a chance to learn and grow.
Pursue your dream now like your life depends on it. Allow your trade and
talents to be refined by examining what sets your purpose apart from
that of others. Do this every step of the way. Each new season of your
life brings about new revelations in your dream. Don't resent the work
this journey requires. Revel in it.

     I recently met a dear lady making her debut in the photography
world. For eighteen years she worked at home, dedicating her time to
raising and serving her family. After decades of thinking only of others,
she found herself at a crossroads. The children had all left home and
she was left to question the purpose of her newfound freedom. This
can be a pitfall. What do you do when all you have ever known has run
its course and you find yourself in a new phase, and possibly lost and
restless? Weather you have been in school or working an eight-to-five
desk job, changing direction can be intimidating.

I would say this: All paths in life run parallel. The toughest decision isn't to change your path, but rather to embrace where you are, right now. Realize that your current path and your purpose path are only a few choices apart. You will experience different work in the many seasons of your life and likewise you will see portions of your dream come to life. Use every bit of your prior education, experience, and pent up passion to pursue your next road stronger than ever before.

It's never too late to dedicate your energy to doing what you love.

This searching allowed my new friend to focus, for the first time, on her creative passions. Photographing her family had always energized her, but until she was pushed, she didn't think much of it. All of these years she had unknowingly been training to be one of the most impactful family photographers I have ever seen. She approaches her work with passion and enthusiasm that not only touches her clients deeply, but sets her creative eye above seasoned veterans.

When Gene and I set out on our journey, we were chasing our dream to design and build furniture. We didn't have much, but we made a choice to chase after that big idea. Buying a shop's worth of materials and tools wasn't in the budget, nor did we have a shop to use them in. So we began by seizing the opportunities we did have. Restoring existing furniture, otherwise forgotten, was a practical and rewarding approach to our dream.

RATHER THAN BEING DISCOURAGED BY WHERE YOU ARE NOT, BEGIN TO FOCUS SOLELY ON WHAT IT IS YOU WANT TO SPEND THE REST OF YOUR LIFE BUILDING. DURING THIS FIRST YEAR YOU WILL BE REFINED BY YOUR WILLINGNESS TO LEARN AND SEIZE OPPORTUNITIES.

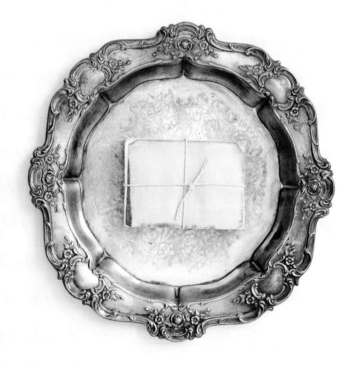

On our first antiquing trip, we took $1,000 dollars and our old Toyota van to a Nashville flea market. The road to that market felt like the gateway to our independence. We were like two kids, buying and haggling to stay within our budget. We spent the drive home dreaming of the different ways we would restore our rescues. We paid $75 to $200 dollars for each piece and after our restoration process, they sold for $300 to $600 each. It was a start. Those founding steps changed our lives. I sharpened my skills as a finisher and learned to love the parallel direction of our dream. For us, it didn't make any matter whether we'd brought $1,000 to the market that day or $100. That singular success, when repeated, led to more successes. Those successes were the foundation for Amy Howard at Home.

ASK YOURSELF

Where does your dream fit into your life?

What opportunities exist right now to use your talents?

What can you do now to pursue your dream?

Committed

There is a definite fear factor when you are choosing to go after your dream. I acknowledge that dear maker, I do.

The fear of not being able to provide the money you and your family need. The fear that maybe you will fail to see your dream come to life. The fear that people will think you have lost your mind or worse, they will not believe in you. These fears will paralyze you if you allow them that authority. However, there exists a fear that will weigh heavier and cut far deeper than even those. The fear of regret. What if you never choose to pursue your dreams and your purpose, but instead choose to live a life riddled with regrets?

The fear of living a lie has to be bigger than the fear of falling on your face.

If you are honest with yourself, you will likely find the fear of pain and failure as the root cause of your hesitation. You can speak your dreams, but the intentional steps to achieve them often feel tortuous. You will always stay a dreamer and never become a doer if you fail to implement measurable choices to get to your dream. What makes you feel more alive, dear maker, playing in the game or sitting on the bench? Most people want their life to be known for something and for having done that something very well. And yet, so many of us, don't embrace the commitment it takes to pursue our dreams.

I like commitment because I like results. A lack of commitment to your dream is a lack of belief in yourself. By not making the decision to commit your choices, your time, your money and your energy to pursuing what will make you the best version of yourself, you are saying your dream isn't worth it. If you are too fearful to be committed, you are allowing yourself to be ruled by that fear. Without purpose, you are living in uncertainty, indifference, insignificance and hopelessness. Fear is not an element of authority, choice is. Taking up the reigns of pursuit will not only boost your confidence, it will inspire those around you. Everyone is designed to pursue the purpose of their dreams.

In his book *Outliers*, journalist and public speaker Malcolm Gladwell describes the roughly 10,000 hours of practice it takes to achieve mastery in a field of study. Through their examination of the lives of high achievers in many fields, psychologists' statistics revealed a direct link between the hours of practice and developing an elite level talent. Natural talent had nothing to do with the levels of achievement. Every person in the studies Gladwell examined either practiced their way to the top or remained mediocre. Dabbling in something is a detriment to excellence. The jack of all trades, but the master of none has never decided to settle on something and study it enough to excel at it.

Land somewhere, dear maker. Start where you are, plant your feet firmly in your purpose, and do what it takes to move forward in excellence. Everyone begins somewhere.

CONSIDER THIS Dear maker, one of the greatest opportunities you can have, is the opportunity to examine your life choices. The push to get real with yourself may seem taxing, but the light on the other end is shining bright with freedom. I would never tell you this is an easy journey, but I will tell you it is an adventure. Remember: your perseverance is fully dependent on what you are feeding yourself.

Right now, I want you to write a detailed letter to your future self. Explain what you are feeling as you have starred your dreams in the face. Write the account of how this experience has compared with the previous prospect of settling forever. Whenever you become discouraged or distracted, read your letter. If nothing else, believe that your dreams are well worth the journey.

When I decided that I had experienced enough of what the path of obligation had to offer and that it was time to pursue my dream, I also had to decide I was all in. My children were still small; I still had to work and provide; but I enrolled in a full-time dual degree program at a local university. I was so hungry to learn the business of using my creativity; it was all worth it. I slept less than I liked. It was hard to keep up, but the fact that I was finally moving forward with my dream kept me going.

There are innumerable avenues you can walk during your lifetime, dear maker. This roadmap doesn't look kindly on compromise. Trust me, your life is worth so much more than settling in misery. No, you don't have to set out to own a multi-million dollar international business operation. You can find satisfaction in any capacity as long as it is in your purpose, your giftings, and your dream. You have been designed to be in the game. Realize that in your lifetime you are either deciding to pursue your purpose or not. The decision to make no decision is still a decision. And you are going to be committed either way. Are you committed to deciding or to settling?

ASK YOURSELF

What is the business of your purpose?

What will be your greatest reward as you pursue that business?

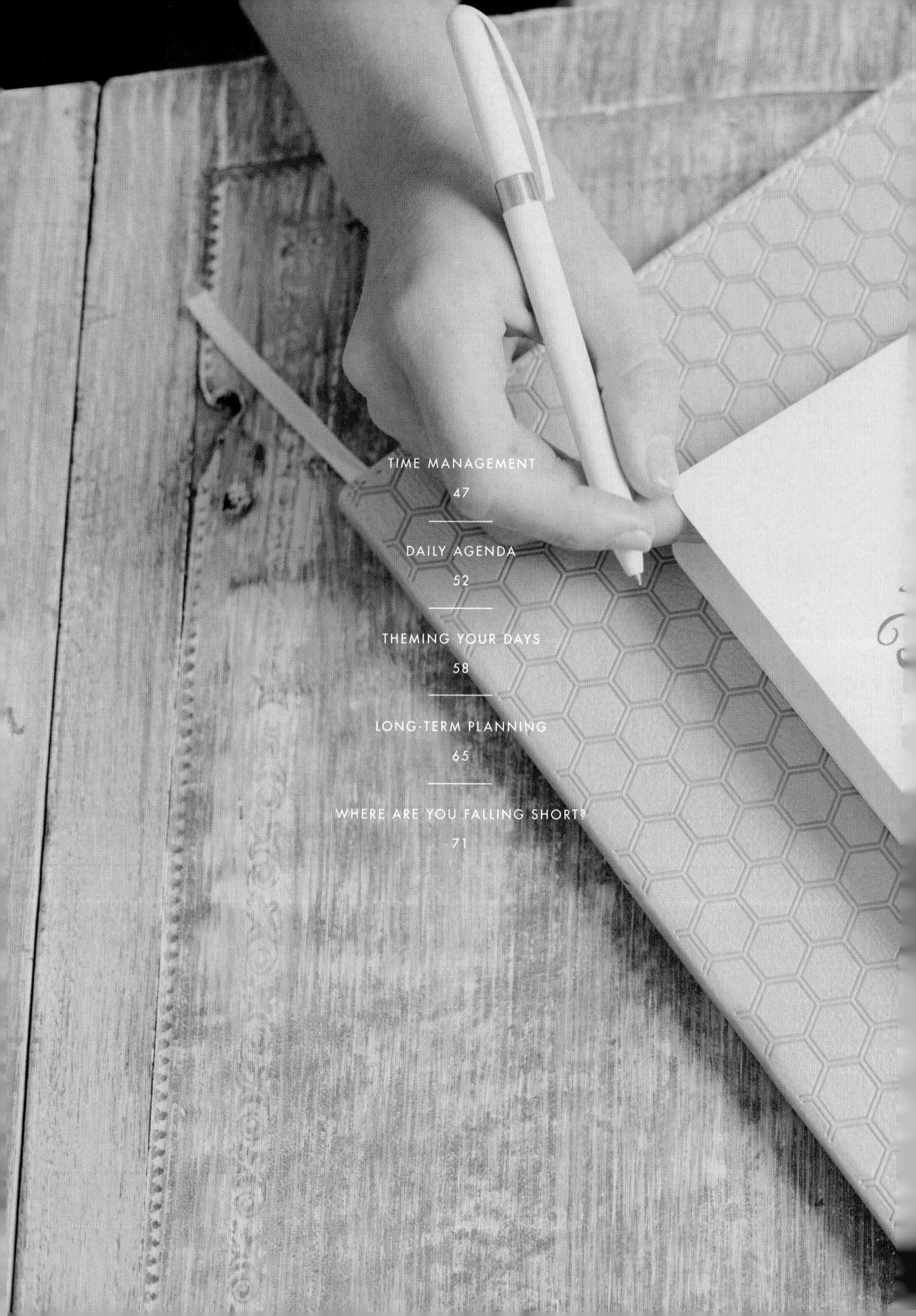

Living with Intention

Time Management

You can always complain you don't have the time to pursue your passion or you have too many tasks to complete before you begin.

These excuses will keep you from your dream. People stay right where they are, even if they're miserable, because they believe they lack the energy to change their lives. Yet, if you look at every decision as an intentional act of moving forward to your purpose, you'd be amazed at the opportunities already in front of you everyday. You just haven't been measuring.

WHERE DOES THE DAY GO?

When I'm teaching our in-house vendor workshops, I challenge the participants to write down everything they do, every 15 minutes, for three days. This may sound like a large undertaking, but the results will spell out where your precious purpose-chasing energy is being wasted. I always recommend analyzing the accounts after, rather than during, the three days. Reflecting back on what you have done with that cluster of time will have an irrefutable impact on you. Sometimes this is the most eye-opening exercise you can ever do.

I believe the answer to your lack of results, thus far, is found in the choices you make, every minute.

We use too much of our free time browsing social media, playing app games, searching the internet, and watching television. These tasks, however vital they seem, should be categorized as idle luxuries: doing nothing or not of use. Watching two hours of television every day won't make you happier, smarter, wealthier, or even more relational. You will have simply checked out, shut down, and made no difference in your life or in the lives around you. If you believe you don't have time to implement change, exam how you spend the time you do have.

EDIT AND FOCUS

To edit is to change, correct, condense, and remove unnecessary or inappropriate content. To focus is to pay attention or become able to see clearly. Plenty of people, priorities, and projects should not be edited out. They are part of the enriching fullness of your life. However, if you discover anything wasteful or unproductive blocking the clear path to achieving your dream, edit it out. Allow yourself the luxury of freely focusing on the tasks that will lead you to your purpose.

CONSIDER THIS I would like to invite you to complete a 3-day challenge. This task, by far, has provided me with my greatest wake-up call. In order to complete your challenge you will need a pocket-sized notebook, a pen and ample amounts of endurance. The challenge is as follows: For three days, write down everything you do every fifteen minutes. That's it. I have found the most effective way to complete this challenge is with the help of a timer. Make sure to write the accounts of your day in real-time. Do not go back and try to remember the last hour or two.

At the end of those three days, review everything you did. You will see, in great detail, how you are living your days, minute by minute. Not only will you be astonished by how you use your time, you will more than likely be deeply moved to make some major changes. Rarely are we intentional with our days without first coming to a revelation about our losses. By the end of the challenge, you will have taken leaps towards growing in excellence.

The most promising opportunities can be seized in your <u>singular</u> <u>steps</u>.

I have a rule that at the beginning of each day, I spend forty-five minutes of quiet time to gather my thoughts. I desperately want to answer my dinging phone, but I choose to ignore it and start my day off with intent. Some of my most productive times are alone at my home, before I go into the office. When I am exercising, I'm not zoned out, I'm listening to a podcast, an audio book, or a TED talk. I schedule at least an hour of reading a day. I see it as my 'me-time'. I'm choosing to enrich my life to the fullest, every chance I get. I choose to focus on my growth rather than live as a slave to mindless waste. I have lived fifty years of my life this way and I believe it has been the key to guarding against foolish decisions. We can never have a do-over. Days are here and gone, never to return. I am choosing to treat every day as a gift.

Dear maker, you are what you feed yourself and you will eventually begin to pursue what you have been fed. With each intentional choice, you are growing in excellence. Pull yourself away from those distractions or you will never gain the discipline to grow. Of course this takes hard work, but your dreams are only obtained with intention. Going about your days by happenstance is a waste. It does not take an entire life overhaul to end up with a successful business. The most promising opportunities can be seized in your singular steps.

ASK YOURSELF

Do your challenge results align with achieving your dreams? How and how not?

What is the number one time waster in your life right now?

How can you move towards replacing that waste?

Daily Agenda

The secret to your success can be found in your daily agenda. Likewise, the guarantee of your failure is in the absence of one.

Most of us don't like the word Discipline, it can sound confining. Disciplining yourself to write a daily agenda, however, turns living with intent into a tangible and practical goal. Choosing every step of your day with intent and integrity gives you more freedom than there ever will be in the trap of wastefulness. You only think you are living in freedom as you leisurely go about your day.

Dear maker, if you aren't consciously choosing your steps, your steps are choosing for you.

How many people wake up with no written plan of accomplishments each day? Too many extremely capable people never experience success because they never had a plan. What happens when you fail to center your choices around an agenda to meet your goals? Your goals don't get met. Never underestimate the power of writing everything down.

What does it mean to live everyday with intention? Living with intention is living in the conscious understanding that today is a gift. We don't know about tomorrow. You are given twenty-four hours at a time, that's what you can handle. Plan like you have forever, but live like you only have today. Intention is about how you are treating today and realizing that a day lived well requires a plan. Scheduling everything, even your play time, every day will free you to live to the fullest of your capabilities. When you plan, nothing falls through the cracks, nothing is deemed wasteful. Even leisure time becomes time spent with intent.

PLAN YOUR DAY HOUR
BY HOUR. LAYING OUT
YOUR RESPONSIBILITIES IN
WRITING WILL HELP YOU SEE
THAT YOU CAN ACTUALLY
ACCOMPLISH EVERYTHING
NEEDED. IF ANYTHING ON
THE LIST DOESN'T FLOW
WITH THE REST OF THE DAILY
TASKS, TRY TO MOVE IT TO
A DIFFERENT DAY. THERE IS
NO NEED TO ENSUE STRESS
WHEN IT IS UNNECESSARY.

A daily agenda can look something like this:

TODAY'S DATE   June 12

6:00–6:30	wake up / coffee / priority time
6:30–7:00	walk
7:00–7:30	shower
7:30–8:00	check email
8:00–8:30	social media updates (pinterest, IG, facebook...)
8:30–9:30	interview customer service person
9:30–10:30	meet with new banker
10:30–11:30	update website / check emails
11:30–12:30	take photos of new product
	– write blog posts for tomorrow
12:30–1:30	lunch + phone calls

Start with your daily to-do list. Write down everything you need to accomplish each day. Spending time with friends and family and even checking emails and social media can all go onto the list. Generally your responsibilities will fall into three categories: People, Places and Priorities. Then, hour by hour place each task into a time slot. That's it. Everything you need to accomplish in your twenty-four hours is accounted for and waiting to be crossed off.

As a creative person you might be known for being scatterbrained, forgetful, or flaky. When you are planning your days and living with intent, those tendencies are no longer a crutch. Your intentional-ism will begin to grow and permeate through your entire life. I carry my yellow legal pad and my beloved black sharpie with me everywhere. Key information and last-minute additions collect over the day. I review my notes in the evening to ensure tomorrow's plans are fed from today's runoff. I always apply the edit and focus rule to these new needs. Do all of these new tasks align with my overall mission? If not, they are edited out. This investment in your own personal excellence will take you from lost and helpless to a trustworthy leader of the pack.

ASK YOURSELF

When was the last time you consistently worked from a daily agenda?

What will be the most freeing aspect of implementing an hourly to-do list?

Theming Your Days

*Every step of your daily agenda must encompass
your strategy for accomplishing your mission.*

The method of theming your days provides the framework for obtaining results. Theming your days frees you up to say, "No I don't have time to meet this Monday, I generally schedule meetings on Thursdays. Can you meet on Thursday?" You are able to plan and choose your tasks guilt free, knowing that everything will get done.

Not everything has to happen today.

To theme your days is to allow each day its own target. Every day will have a full set of tasks no matter what, but instead of planning at random, each to-do list aligns with the theme of its day. Otherwise you might find yourself scrambling to fit everything in. Scrambling brings exhaustion and burnout. Theming provides order and peace of mind.

Theming isn't about saying no to anything, but rather growing disciplined in your focus.

A themed weekly agenda might look something like this:

DAILY THEME *company goals, planning*	*new product development, implementation*	*social media, blog posts*	*growth, partnerships, alliances*	*financial & imp*
MON	TUES	WED	THURS	FRI
1	2	3	4	5
meeting with team	*in studio*	*blog about latest product*	*coffee with fellow entrepreneur*	*study fin she*
8	9	10	11	12
release press copy				

Every Monday we come together for team meetings. We cover our mission for the week, along with the details of accomplishing it. Tuesday, Wednesday and Thursdays are set aside for our in-house workshops. Teaching and pouring into the participants is my focus. Friday we choose to have date night: our time to refuel and focus on each other. No matter what my week has been like, I can look forward to down time with my husband. Saturday is my recharge with family day. Sunday is my time to start planning for the next week.

It will take trial and error to find your sweet spot. Don't be afraid to test out and adjust your themes. A few rules of thumb: Take time for your family. Don't feel guilty about putting them first when they need you. Learn to cut off at a certain time each day. Set aside time to rest. You will be much more refreshed going into your next work days. Last minute changes, interruptions and additional tasks will always pop up. Theming isn't about saying no to anything, but rather growing disciplined in your focus.

ASK YOURSELF

What are some themes you could introduce into your daily agenda?

Are you theming portions of your week already without realizing?

Name all of the areas theming will help you retain focus in.

Long-Term Planning

A comprehensive strategy builds an indisputable foundation for your future success.

Long term planning looks ahead into the next week, the next month, and hopefully the years to come to lay out the future of your mission. There has to be a measurement component to every one of your daily plans if you want to experience long term success in your dream. Start by writing down every goal, need, and responsibility you're facing this year. All goals, even your personal ones, must be articulated and given a deadline to keep you accountable.

Some practical long-term breakdowns include:

TIME

How many hours you can realistically give over to your new idea? Do you need to invest in classes or workshops to sharpen your skills?

MONEY

How much do you need to be fully supported? What practical needs does your dream have? Do you need to buy equipment, tools or materials? Do you need to be able to afford retail or office space? How much can you afford to spend on your first investment purchase?

What are your workload goals for this upcoming year? How do you plan to promote your new endeavors? Are you willing to offer free or discounted promotions in the beginning? At what point will you raise your prices? If you have another job, how many extra hours can your workload support and when will you be able to transition to part time?

HELP

Do you need to meet with a lawyer for any legal advice? Does your work require permits, contracts, or licensing? Do you need to meet with a CPA before the new tax year? What team members would you like to hire this next year?

Once you see all the details laid out, you will be able to break down immediate responsibilities and long term goals. What you can't achieve tomorrow should be considered a long-term goal. Plan your strategies to meet the next year's responsibilities and goals in measurable steps. Make sure your plans are attainable, practical, and achievable. Align your choices and themes so your vision, passion, mission and purpose will highlight your personal roadmap to growth.

LIFELONG		SHORT-TERM (3wks - 3mo)
GOAL / COST / COMPLETION DATE		GOAL / COST / COMPLETION DATE
1		1
2		2
3		3

DREAM GOALS

LONG-TERM (1-5 Years)		MEDIUM-TERM (3mo - 1 yr)
GOAL / COST / COMPLETION DATE		GOAL / COST / COMPLETION DATE
1		1
2		2
3		3

IF YOUR LIFESTYLE DOESN'T
REFLECT YOUR LONG-TERM
GOALS, IT IS TIME TO MAKE
SOME CHANGES. LOOKING
AHEAD EXPOSES WHERE YOU
ARE FALLING SHORT TODAY.
SET YOUR FUTURE DREAMS
IN MOTION BY MAKING
THEM PRIORITY AND
PLANNING FOR THEM NOW.

Plan everything enough in advance realistically and, not by squeezing in. Your long term plans (3 month, 6 months, yearly) won't amount to anything if your daily agenda isn't designed to get you there.

Over a span of time, small steps progress into large leaps.

What you do every day makes all the difference for the big picture. Chipping away and being consistent with your mission ensures your long term success. Never be afraid to edit and focus throughout your long-term plans. It will always come back to the intentional choice to accomplish your dream.

ASK YOURSELF

What daily goals can you implement to meet the mission of your big idea?

What long-term goals can you implement to meet the mission of your big idea?

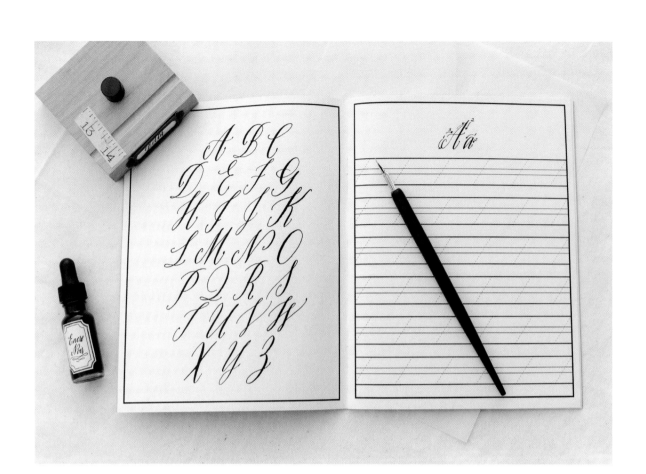

Where Are You Falling Short?

After examining your daily activities, I'm sure you've found places where you're falling short.

Each of us feels helplessly out of order in one or two areas of our life. Most of us feel we could either be healthier or better with our money and time. If you're going to struggle with anything as a creative, it's going to be discipline.

Non-essential things must be eliminated from your daily routine if you want to see measurable change.

Get rid of anything that distracts or takes away from your goals. Pulling back from your loose spending of money, time, or calories will give you the freedom to do more. Trimming the fat and ceasing the mindless wasting of your energy will solidify your pursuit of excellence. Dear maker, this is relevant in all your personal and business choices. You can have money, you can have time, and you can have success. It's all in the details.

Statistically, Americans spend an average of three hours per day on social media. In a decade you will have lost one year and three months of your life to nothingness. Where would you be right now, if you were allowed to take a year off and just focus on your dream? You have the time, dear maker, every wasted hour. Those small "luxuries" compound into large losses over the course of your life. Accounting for every detail will show you where your energy is not only going, but where your irreplaceable days are slipping through the cracks.

I invite you to take a 21-day challenge. Choose the area of your life where you struggle the most. Take the next 21 days to focus on what it looks like to take control. Whether your weakness is in spending money, putting off tasks, eating poorly, or wasting time, within these 21 days you will see through the veil of your excuses. If you save $20 a day you will have made over $400. If you cut out 150 calories a day, you will have lost a pound. If you only spend fifteen minutes on social media a day, you will have reclaimed over sixty-five hours of your wasted time. Imagine those calculations over the course of a year. My hope is that this model will become your new way of living.

CONSIDER THIS Right now where you are, make a list of the areas in your life where you need to offer more disciplinary focus. What habits have you allowed in your daily routine that offer little or no benefit? Most shortcomings were founded in neglect. It is never a case of sheer luck when excellence is attained. No one is simply born ready for the big game. You graduate to it.

The 21-day challenge is meant to serve you and your future. During these next days, you will be able to pamper your greatest needs with the focus they deserve. No more rushing around and forgetting about yourself. These next few days are about becoming the best version of yourself. It is exactly what we all desire!

You can have money, you can have time, and you can have success. It's all in the details.

You can be disciplined, dear maker – it's a choice. Practice reviewing your choices at the end of each day, week, month, quarter, and year. Be honest about where you're falling short and revel in what you have accomplished. It is about being intentional with your days and knowing that you have a choice in what you are going to accomplish or not accomplish. This journey is about investing in your personal excellence. I guarantee you this will lead to opportunities you never anticipated.

ASK YOURSELF

What area of waste in your life will you focus on cutting out for 21-days?

What do you hope to accomplish during your 21-day challenge?

What do you imagine will be your reward?

Come back at the end of your challenge and compare your results to your expectations.

The Business
of Your Dreams

Competitive Landscape

Nothing is new. Everything is a reinvention. Whether it's a canvas painting or a piece of furniture, it's all been done before.

We have a rule of thumb in business: Don't be afraid to do what's already been done; do it better.

You will learn new things about yourself and about your business every step of this journey, dear maker. To focus on your best, you must uncover it. In his book *Good to Great*, author Jim Collins expounds his theory of the hedgehog concept. Greatness comes from focus. Simplify your mission by honing in on the talents and passions specific only to you. Focus will set you apart from your competition. Collins offers three steps for finding focus. First, understand and articulate what your central passion is. Second, understand and articulate what you can do better than anyone around you. Third, understand and uncover your economic drive. What will propel your profits? As you allow your three steps to overlap, you will see what sets you above everyone else, and gives you the most potential in the world.

What you are
deeply passionate
about

HEDGEHOG

Where your
true mission
and disciplines
should be.

What you can
be the best
in the world at

What drives
your economic
engine

Being an art history major, I loved the beautifully painted pieces of furniture filling our decorative heritage. When we began Amy Howard Collection, I looked at the factory-produced furniture around me and saw a focus for my passion. The furniture market was missing what I could offer – the touch of an artisan. There was nothing mass-produced about our home furnishings. My drive for creativity and excellence ensured our pieces stood apart in texture and appearance. By listening to our clients, we understood that the quality of our finishes were what they couldn't find anywhere else. Our rescued furniture was my canvas. Nina Campbell, a renowned interior designer from the United Kingdom, walked into my showroom one day. She looked around and said, "My dear, your furniture isn't like furniture at all. Your furniture is like jewelry." That was my mission. I wanted every item I designed to not only contribute to a beautiful space, but to stand alone as a gem. Our finishes were our hedgehog. What set us apart was the fact that every piece of furniture was touched by an artist's hands.

What you are offering has to be so great that it will pull your target audience away from their previous purchasing choices.

You want them to make what you are offering their priority. Always take your customers feedback to heart. They'll be your greatest ally when competition arrives. What you hear will open your eyes to where you can improve and how you can set yourself above the rest throughout the life of your business.

A SIMPLE HEDGEHOG TEST WOULD BE TO ASK YOUR CLOSEST FRIENDS TWO QUESTIONS: 1) WHAT ATTRIBUTES DO THEY THINK OF WHEN THEY HEAR YOUR NAME? 2) WHAT SKILLS DO THEY SEE IN YOU AND YOUR BUSINESS THAT ARE UNIQUE?

What sets you apart is what are you will be known for. Seeing how you can take over your market and seizing that opportunity will be what sets your business ideas ablaze. When you know you can produce something the world needs, your drive grows that much stronger. If you are still unsure about what your hedgehog is, take more time to analyze and practice your skills. Allow these first steps to be the learning curve turning you towards a successful business.

ASK YOURSELF

What can you see in the world that others cannot, dear maker?

What need in the world ignites your passion?

What is it that you can do the best, that no one can replace you?

What can you do with your passion to make it profitable?

Business Plan

*Facts, details, the torture of having to sit down
and account for everything; this is the area where
you as a creative are likely to struggle the most.*

The average small business owner has never created a business plan. Quite often, the mistake of never writing it out derives from the belief that unless you are going to apply for a business loan, it isn't a necessary step. A detailed business plan isn't just for the occasion of a loan, this is the indisputable framework your business runs on. Employee information, historical documentation, financial accounts, detailed explanations; all of your concrete information needs to be stored in one organized place. Once completed, you will find it becomes a source of confidence as well.

> You not only have a good idea, your detailed plan shows that it is concrete and ready to be executed.

This step will also save you from the chaos associated with lacking necessary information. The day I set out to write my business plan, I went into lockdown for 8 hours. I was determined to flesh out every detail until I had developed my idea into a legitimate business. If I didn't know an answer, I researched it. If I didn't have the information yet, I developed my ideas until the answers was born. I left no question unacknowledged. The importance for me was found in the reality that I was going to have to sell everybody on my idea. No one is going to believe in you if you don't believe in it yourself. The practicality of your passion can be found in your willingness to account for every detail.

A healthy business plan will always be based on your hedgehog. It spells out exactly how much the business of your dreams stands to make and your projected financial performance through profit and loss. A business plan allows loan officers, clients, associates, and future partners to understand what you offer and how you will go about producing it. Type out all of your answers in a detailed presentable format.

1) DESCRIBE WHAT YOUR BUSINESS DOES
   a) What does the market need that you are going to be solving?
   b) Create 7 reasons why you are going to be successful within your market. These need to be fact-based and arguable. Examples:
      • There is a $718.5 billion DIY industry. Within our upcycling market, 60% of all of the rescued furniture is used in children's rooms. Our paint is the only naturally methanol free product in the market and it doesn't have to be sealed.
      • Our line is a lifestyle brand, not just a singular product. We are showing our customers how to upstyle, not just upcycle.
   c) Why are customers going to buy your product rather than the others already offered?

2) SHOW YOUR FINANCIAL PROJECTIONS
   a) Describe how you are going to financially back up your plans by reverse engineering your profit and loss figures.
      • How much do you need to sell in order to make a profit after your costs and overhead are accounted for?
      • Substantiate this by accounting for every cost associated with starting your business. (ie. website, branding, lease, equipment, product costs, supplies, etc.)
   b) How much money do you need to bring in each month in order to meet those projections and earn a profit?

The practicality of <u>your passion</u> can be found in your willingness to account for every detail.

3) BUSINESS OVERVIEW
   a) List the following in detail, complete with addresses and relationship history:
      • Location
      • Formation (LLC, Sole proprietorship, etc.)
      • Partners and participating parties. (List contact information and job descriptions)

4) BUSINESS ANALYSIS
   a) Write out a description of your competitive market and the trends within that market. Describe as though you are educating someone.
   b) What will set you apart from the other leaders in that market?

5) NAME YOUR TARGET CUSTOMERS
   a) Describe how you are going to identify their needs.
   b) Describe how you will meet those needs.

6) MARKETING PLAN
   a) Describe your products or services.
   b) Describe how you will position your brand in the marketplace.
   c) Display your logo, packaging, branding, etc.

7) PROMOTIONAL PLAN
   a) Describe your promotional plan for the next 3 months, 6 months and year.
   b) List the tactics you will use to ensure your customers know about you. ie: Press releases, social media accounts, local community involvement, philanthropic associations and giving, etc. You must have a presence that people are going to be seeing on a regular basis.
   c) Backup you current social media standing. ie: 6,000 Facebook likes, 2,000 blog followers, etc.
   d) Create a plan to double your followers by next year.
      • What other companies can you co-brand with in the future?
      • Create a calendar of when you are going to be issuing business news and press releases.

8) OPERATIONAL PLAN
   a) Name the processes your team members are going to execute daily.
   b) How are you going to achieve success everyday? This is the practical breakdown of your core policies.

9) MANAGEMENT TEAM
   a) Who are the key people that are going to help you reach your goals and implement your business plan? These are the people that are in the day to day operation. Those that understand the goal at hand and can execute your business model.
   b) Document these employees education, accolades, accomplishments & successes.
   c) What day to day goals is your team needing meet?
   d) What daily processes do your team members follow?

10) FINANCIAL PLAN

    a)   Describe how you are going to generate revenue.

    b)   List a summary of your financial projections for your business' fiscal year.

    c)   How much money will you need this year and what is it earmarked for? Examples:

- Building a website: $3500 flat
- Lease $4500 a month
- Sign $1300 flat
- Branding $1900 flat
- POS system $45 a month
- Computers $5500 flat
- FurniturelSupplies $8,000 flat
- Attorney $130 a month
- Accountant $200 a month
- Savings $500 a month

11) APPENDIX

    a)   Summarize your products, financial standing, patents and income statements through profit & loss.

    b)   Close with a synopsis as to why you would be great to invest in.

After you have completed the detailed breakdown of your business plan, create a one-page summary. This should be a brief but concise overview; keep it short and succinct. This will serve as a quick reference guide in your day to day routine. The best way to extract value from your business plan is to use it as an ongoing management tool. To do this, revisit and revise your business plan constantly to reflect current conditions and the new information that you've collected as your business grows.

Budget & Investments

Investment can be scary. The word rolls off the tongue with a distinguished tone, but when you're talking about your own money, it can inspire some anxiety.

People hesitate to invest because they either don't know where to focus, or they don't believe in the long term value of what they're doing. If you don't believe in yourself, who will? You're either setting yourself up for growth or you're choosing not to grow. Dear maker, if you don't see a future for your efforts or don't believe in your own business enough to invest in it yourself, why would new clientele, let alone a bank do so for you?

As our furniture sales grew in the first year, we saw the need for a showcase venue. We scoured the city and found a beautiful historic home zoned commercial in the heart of the arts district. Demographically, it was right on target. I remember praying to be able to just get past $10,000 in our bank account. We knew though, that without having a shop, our business would not survive. We took a leap of faith and purchased that small home for $94,000. Each of the rooms had a theme, a small sampling of our abilities and offerings. Every inch of that venue felt like a dream home. As soon as our clients walked through the door every sight, every smell, every flower display, and every texture said one thing: Amy Howard furniture is set apart.

Some costs must always be considered when choosing where to invest. Salaries, rents, inventories, maintenance, supplies, fees for extended members of your team (bookkeeper, CPA, legal advisor), and a media budget must be a part of your plan. Your business cannot stand on any less than 50% profit. After you account for costs, overhead, and the time it takes to produce your work, the process won't survive on anything less. Every dollar in sales can build you up and lead you to your dream life, but profits aren't free-flowing cash. Reinvest the money you make back into your business for at least a year. This will speed up the transition into full-time work.

But what if your dream work doesn't produce the income to support your next level of growth? Enter your seven revenue streams.

An average entrepreneur will always have seven streams of revenue they can use within their passions to broaden their income.

As an entrepreneur you are responsible for sustaining your welfare. You won't have a reliable paycheck if you don't chase after it. If your product sales have a slow month, you will always have extra self-sustaining income from your other streams. When dreaming up the different ways you could break off your offerings to clients, remember to think very specific. Generalized work won't catch people's attention as much as a specifically tailored service that fits someone's immediate needs.

SMALL BUSINESSES NEED
FINANCIAL PLANNING
ADVICE FROM AN
INVESTOR JUST AS LARGE
CORPORATIONS DO.
GAINING INSIGHT FROM
AN INVESTOR FOR A FEW
HOURS A YEAR IS NOT
ONLY AFFORDABLE, IT CAN
PREVENT UNFORESEEN
HARDSHIPS.

- Workshops (In-house and on-location)
- Printed how-to guides
- Membership programs
- Product sales
- Private in-home services
- Custom commissioned work
- Build a team to send out in your place
- Renting space out for meetings

Once we established a reliable debt to income ratio, we were free to look at every design we offered and break it down into a formula. I knew how long it took to make each item and the costs involved with the material and labor. I recorded every single step and implemented them into a timed sequence. From cutting the wood to prepping and painting, it was our very own custom assembly line. Pricing your products should eventually be centered around not only the cost of your materials, but the paid time it takes to produce it. Knowing exactly how long it takes you to do everything will be the only way you can budget to the penny.

Once you establish yourself as a reliable business owner, you will find opportunities to grow. Knowing your market opportunities and allowances will open avenues for investing more in your business. As your confidence builds, you will make even bolder investments and your operation will grow. In the right context, stepping out boldly will get you to the next level. The fear is not in the stepping out of your comfort zone, but in the discipline it takes to sustain the steps of your success.

I have encountered business owners so fearful of taking investment leaps into their own business that they are paralyzed into not making decisions at all. Most were well established in their client loyalty and ready for that next level of growth. You are the only visionary for your business. You are going to have to trust yourself in this journey. Self-trust is going to be your greatest ally through every step, especially in growth. Given my experience, my question would be: Why not choose to grow?

ASK YOURSELF

What investment opportunities are in front of you right now?

Name 5 of your long term investment goals.

What intentional choice are your making to free your business up for investment?

Calling Cards

The very place your potential clients will look for their first impression could very well be your greatest weakness.

When you tell people about your new business they will ask "Do you have a business card?" or "What is your website?" Your email, website, and social media accounts are your calling cards. The logo and name you choose has to tell people who you are and what you do. Every display has to draw people in.

When you are in your planning process, look at the brands that draw you in. What makes them stand apart in your eyes? Study their color and font choices. Why do their ad posts speak to you? How does their website make you feel? Be inspired by them and see how you can use that same specialized approach to inspire your audience in your promotional materials. The typography, colors, and imagery of your name and logo will need to paint a picture for your potential clients. Always tailor your design to your target audience rather than your own taste. This process needs to be the most thought out piece of work you have ever done.

Always tailor
your design
to your <u>target</u>
<u>audience</u>
rather than
your own
taste.

I believe it is important in the creative process to come up with a tagline as well as a clearly defined name. Your tagline will not only support your company name, but weed out ambiguity. Invite some of your most creative friends, as well as someone who is going to work with you in your business, to a creative brainstorming session. Have plenty of post it notes and sharpies. Shut all doors and turn off all phones and emails. The only electronic I would have would be a thesaurus website to find descriptive words to tell your story.

Allow yourself to focus on your future.

I spent $14,000 on my initial website design. We later made revisions and the final investment totaled upwards of $25,000. To large corporations this would have been a bargain. However, to someone trying to get their business off the ground, that was a lot of cash. Sadly, many people don't realize the importance of a professionally designed website and jump on a DIY service to build one themselves. While great template and domain services are available, your web space needs an artistic composition to draw every eye to the product and the story behind your business. If you decide to build your website through a DIY service, I recommend hiring a web designer and branding specialist to at least review and consult you on any necessary modifications.

I made sure that all of our photography told our viewers a story of elegance and luxury. I was fortunate enough to build my own homes and hand chose each brick, piece of hardware, and color. I created a home that evoked the Amy Howard Collection brand. Most of my photo shoots were in my homes. They were not staged; they were how I lived. I told the story of how to have a dinner party and how to decorate for the holidays. Every item could be found in our Amy Howard Collection line. My lifestyle inspired my website and my website traffic fed my furniture sales.

LESS IS MORE

Simple rules such as keeping all of your contacts and handles under the same name will allow new clients to find you easily. Your Facebook, Instagram, Twitter and blog posts should all feed into each other and be on the same schedule. Each account will support the other and eventually lead the viewers back to your website. Think of the main bullet points that you want your customer to see and have them on the front page of all of your sites. Easy navigation and well placed links are going to keep them coming back.

ASK YOURSELF

Are you happy with your current brand representation?

What are three areas of advertising you are strong in?

What part of your web presence could be improved upon?

You Are Your Brand

Your brand is what you stand for, the mission you want to get across, and who you are in the process.

Dear maker, when you are passionate about your pursuits, people will buy into you before they buy into your mission. The market wants to own and participate in something with heart and a memorable story. Customers want to invest in something with soul. When you display your passion and drive to pursue a greater purpose, your audience will see you as someone they want to support and then emulate.

As a maker, you have to be willing to come out of your box enough to tell someone what you have made and why it will make a difference in their lives. What it means to you will inspire them to share those same views. I have always designed furniture based on what I would want to own myself. I cannot create something I would not want to have in my own home. As I planned out my products and services, I also had to think about how my customers lived, where they traveled, what they liked, what they read, and where else they shopped.

EVERY CHOICE YOU MAKE FOR YOUR BRAND PLATFORM WILL SUPPORT YOUR MISSION. THE GOAL IS TO HAVE SOMEONE THINK OF YOUR MOST SPECIALIZED OFFERING UPON THE MENTION OF YOUR NAME. WHAT DO YOU THINK OF WHEN YOU HEAR THE NAME NIKE? DISNEY? YOURS?

Our brand has always been about crafting a beautiful life. The day-to-day display of that mission is found in our ambiance. From the music we played to our delivery schedule, we made sure we maintained the authority in luxurious living. I set aside an ample amount of our budget to provide our shop with everything you would want in your home. When customers walked into my showroom, the music was playing, the candles were burning, and the friendly faces were welcoming everyone in. Everyone wanted their home to feel like an Amy Howard Collection showroom. I spent a fortune on flowers. Every vignette was adorned with enchanting foliage. Our window displays were over the top. Every item and accent was purposely placed to draw in our target audience. Our brand and mission were consistent through every choice and process we implemented. People were willing to pay the artisan price tag because they saw that it was all hand-made from our hearts. The soul of your company is what sets you apart.

During our first years in business did business as Artisan Studios, but when we went national, people began to want to know who was behind the brand. Remember, people can buy anything but would rather connect with the maker than buy a manufactured relic. Your mission will begin to grow in value as you tell the story that sets you apart. People nowadays are relational. They need a face – a real person behind the brand. Clients willing to continually invest in you want to be reassured of the heart behind your work.

Your brand is supported by how you treat your customers, how you run your daily operations and how you set your mission above mediocrity. You have to be a person of integrity in order for someone to believe in what you sell them. By being trustworthy, you are gaining the loyal repeat patrons that will support your mission for years to come. Dear maker, your mission is what inspires your brand and your brand is you.

ASK YOURSELF

What does your brand stand for?

What have people said to you about what sets your brand apart?

Do they share your vision of your brand's difference?

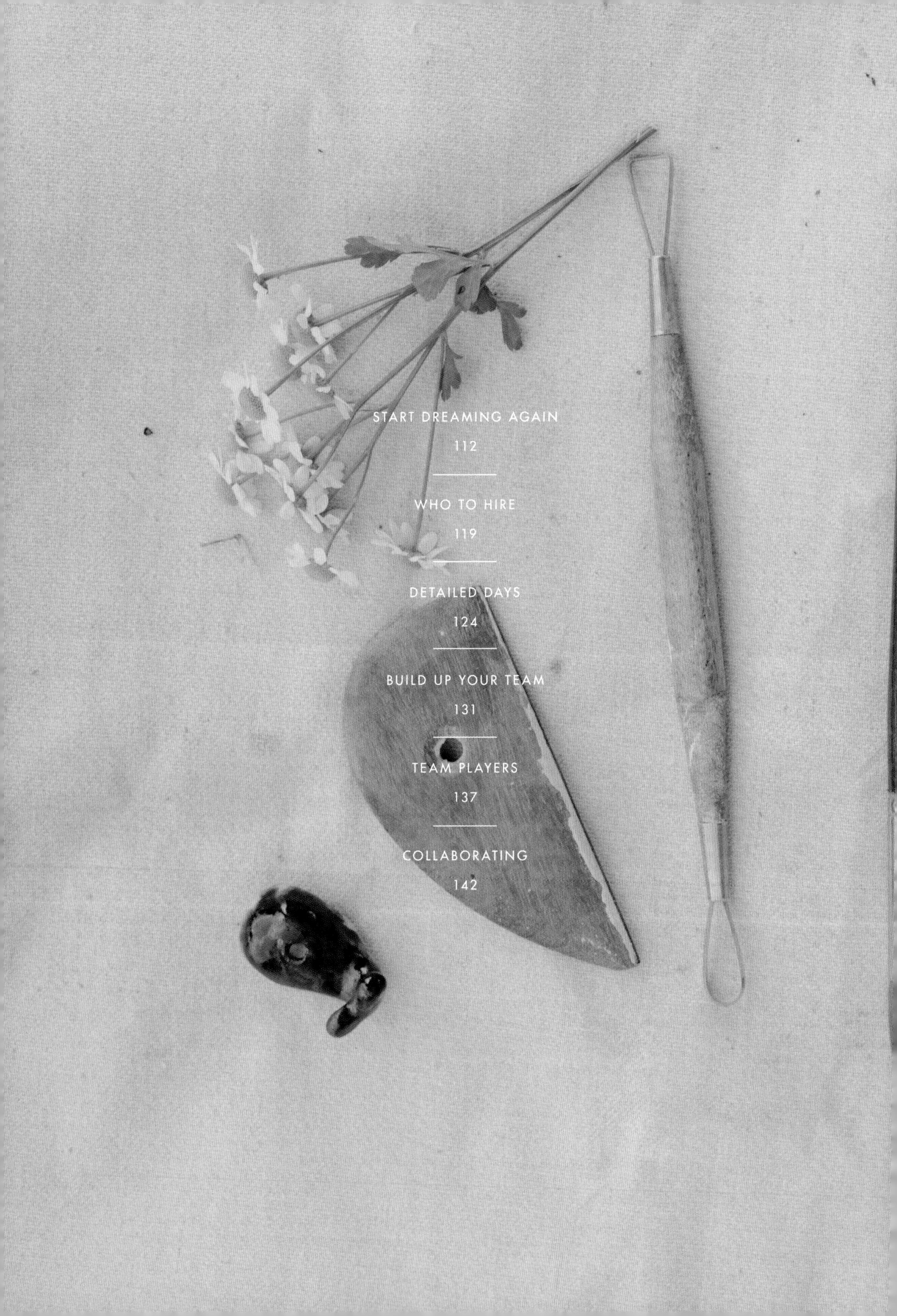

Community

Start Dreaming Again

Close your eyes and dream with me again, dear maker. I want you to dream as though money were no object.

Who would you like to have helping you meet your mission? Write down exactly what you want your team to look like. What would they be responsible for? What would their job descriptions be? What would that free you up to focus on? Draw out sections for each of your 7 streams of revenue. How would you like for each of those operations to break down? Make intentional room to list those responsibilities you enjoy as well as those you would like pass on to others.

Now looking at all the details laid out before you, understand that this is what your business needs to become fully operational. No matter how small or how large of a business you envision, you'll need to feed this information into an organizational chart. All businesses must have every moving part in order to properly function. Even if you only ever have one or two members of your team, you'll still need to list your responsibilities to meet your daily and long-term goals.

It never fails to surprise me how many business owners have never created an organization chart for their responsibilities. You may say, "I am the only member" or "I only have one employee and we do it all." Without an organizational chart, the small but crucial details will begin to fall through the cracks.

Every person involved in your team, including you dear maker, needs to have their responsibilities clearly laid out.

As you grow and bring in more income, you will be able to hire a person to be over each area of the operation. Until then, you have to be creative. Always start by reverse engineering your organizational chart. Start by hiring someone to handle your areas of weakness. Is it bookkeeping, client contacts, or shopping for supplies? Many times you can even hire someone to help you out part time, for a few hours a week.

An organizational chart might look something like this:

Books/Accounting	Marketing	Sales	Customer Se
– AR/AP/HR	– website	– outreach	– relational
– purchasing	– social media	– goal markers	– call reports
– sourcing	– blog	– call reports	– workers/sal
– inventory	– outreach	– opportunities	people
controls	– press releases	– wholesale/	– problem res
– pay roll	– youtube	retail	– materials
– pl/monthly	– photography	– rep groups	represent a
end reports	– SEO	– new customer	sale your b
– budget controls	– look for	outreach	– outreach
– look for areas	growth	– missed	– shipments/
to save money	opportunities	opportunities	emailed
from supplies	– build the brand	– markets/	– looking for
– create BOCs/		conventions	to excel cu
shipping		– sales	expectations
– work with		training/tools	– educate/in

Close your eyes and <u>dream with me again</u>, dear maker. I want you to dream as though money were no object.

CONSIDER THIS Your organizational chart will serve as an invaluable administrative tool as you grow and need to hire help. Remember: You might not have the ability to fill every position just yet, but when the time does come, there will be a plan already set in place to guide you along.

Consultants can be a huge help in those first years. Sometimes in the beginning you simply don't know what your business needs. Hire a professional advisor to look over your business model for a few hours. Have them give you expert advice on where to start and where to focus your attention. Be encouraged. Before you know it, your organizational efforts will have alleviated the stress from unanswered questions. Take advantage of these first stages, dear maker. You are learning so much and setting yourself up for excellence.

ASK YOURSELF

Who would you like to hire during your first year of business?

What creative ways could you make that happen?

What would that first hire mean to your mission?

Who to Hire

When it is time to make your first hire, use your reverse engineered organizational chart.

Your first team member should relieve you where you are weakest and lack enthusiasm. For most of you, this will be a bookkeeper who can also help with customer service. Every hire after that will work in the same reverse order of your needs. Always hire according to the positions outlined on your organizational chart.

THE RIGHT FIT

When I interview a potential team member, I make the DISC personality test my primary determining factor of a candidate's fit for a position. I have never met a person or been in a situation where understanding each participant's personality did not make all the difference. Just like you, the team members you hire need to work according to their strengths and giftings. Through much trial and error, I have recognized the importance of testing everyone and the consequences of not. If they have never tested themselves, they may not even realize they are attempting to submit themselves to an ill-suited position in life.

Years ago I hired a bookkeeper, who by resume standards, was well qualified for the position. Her interview went well. We got along quite nicely in fact. Relationally, she was a 'gold star' employee. But soon I realized that, while she was extremely personable, she was struggling to stay focused and meet her deadlines. What she never knew about herself became a brick-walled obstacle in her work life. Had she or I understood that her strongest personality attribute was relational influence, she could have been thriving in a sales position rather than ashamed of being a terrible bookkeeper.

During the interview process, ask lots of questions and make sure that all team member personalities compliment one another. It is imperative that every member of your team can work together and respectfully appreciate one another. Every employee needs to know their job is about your mission coming to fruition.

If you can't creatively dream as a team, your house is divided and it won't stand.

Never create a job for someone and likewise chose only to hire the team members who help you fill your immediate needs. If you interview someone with whom you would enjoy working, but they don't fill the job requirements, don't hire them. Keep their information for the future. There will likely come a day when your workload does match their skill set.

DON'T BE AFRAID TO GET A NEW MEMBER INVOLVED IN IMPORTANT TASKS ON THEIR FIRST DAY. IF THEY ARE ABLE TO SEE HOW THEIR ROLE IS VITAL TO THE DAILY MISSION, YOU WILL HAVE GAINED A LOYAL MEMBER DEDICATED TO THE GREATER LONG-TERM MISSION.

AGENDA DRIVEN

Agenda driven members will always be the employees you keep long term. I say this in all seriousness, don't hire people who walk slow. Over the past 25 years, the only four people I have had to let go were slow to get the job done, slow to get to work and slow in step. The coinciding factor was that there was never a sense of urgency in their day, in their duty, or in any area of their life for that matter. I watch my interviewees walk to the door, through the office and back out to their car. If they aren't enthused about the potential to work with you, they certainly won't be when they actually have to.

Have your team member's duties and job description in writing. Sit down with them and talk them through every detail. Talk openly about your expectations for them and the business agenda as a whole. Discuss the culture, the environment, and your future plans with them. When your team members feel like they are a meaningful part of a higher purpose, they will work with much more enthusiasm and dedication.

EGOS ARE LEFT AT THE DOOR

As you bring on more staff, some members may feel their position is more important than others simply because they do more. The beauty of a team is that every member is important if they set your mission in motion. The modern workforce is different. People can often work more efficiently from home than they can in an office every day. Your company needs people in a variety of positions. Part-time bookkeepers, members who strictly work from home, and mobile members who travel for sales are all meaningful and necessary.

Every team member will have some decision-making ability within their position. Each team member's emotional quotient will determine how they apply that power. Every member needs to have a certain level of emotional intelligence with the customer base, but even more so with each other. It is imperative that your entire team applies the highest level of self awareness, self regulation, independent motivation, and interpersonal social skills. Plainly said, everyone is going to have to be willing to learn from each other. Employees, like you, must work with integrity. Each person should be able to work within their own giftings and thrive as they were intended.

ASK YOURSELF

Where are you strong in your emotional quotient?

What will you look forward to the most as you grow your team?

Detailed Days

You will need a daily agenda to accomplish your mission, and so will your team.

When you are working to grow your brand, every step must be made with intention. To guard against wasted time and miscommunication, create a framework for every team member's day. Detailing your employees' daily tasks is the practical extension of your organizational chart. Like everything else in your life, it must be written out and concrete if it is going to get it done.

In the first days of Amy Howard Collection, I had every task broken down into a daily checklist that looked something like this:

___Turn all the lights on, including the back
___Open up the cash register
___Turn on the music
___Light the candles
___Open the front door

Our employees not only followed their to-do list, but a daily sales plan as well. Whoever worked the front desk was also in charge of writing invitations to our target audience. The newspaper listed all of the recent property closings in our area. We would write out a letter of congratulations to the new home owners and insert a coupon for our showroom. We would mail out at least ten of these a day. If it needed to be done, it was on the checklist. Each person on your team needs to have a plan written out. Always clearly lay out what each team member needs to accomplish each day and in the weeks ahead.

EVERYONE INVOLVED SHOULD BE WORKING TO REVERSE ENGINEER THEIR WAY TO THE LONG-TERM MISSION OF YOUR BUSINESS. THEIR DAILY STRIDES AND SUCCESSES WILL NOT ONLY BOLSTER YOUR BUSINESS, BUT PROVIDE THEM WITH LONG-TERM SATISFACTION ON YOUR TEAM.

I have had employees tell me they didn't want a job description because they felt it would stifle their creativity. Having a job description does quite the opposite, dear maker. When a member of your team knows your expectations of them, they are free to thrive in that area, not left wondering if they are living up to standards. Every team member should always have the freedom to grow and advance within their position. I recommend re-evaluating your team members' agenda and job descriptions regularly. This will ensure everyone is working to best of their abilities and feels fulfilled doing so.

Most people have to hear something at least seven times in order to commit it to memory or believe it. You can tell a member of your team they need to follow through with a certain task, but if they don't have clarity on the deadline or why that's important, you may never have it done the way you want it. You can't assume anyone is clear about what has to be done. You have to ensure it. What you think and what you want a person to do are two different things. Break down each goal by who will do it and how much time it will take. Start with the end in mind and then lay out a daily roadmap for how to get there. Talk about the who, what, when, where, and why of every planned task you give your team members. By doing so, you are setting a precedent of clarity, open communication, and in turn, training them to be empowered members of your mission.

If you see continued success in your process, write it out in policy form. Until it is written on a daily to do sheet, it doesn't become a policy. The policies that support your mission will then become concrete. Build on your successes, and allow those to become your mission policies. Dear maker, excellence is achieved by repeating your successes over and over again.

How can your daily agenda complement your teams' daily agenda?

How can your team theme their days to meet the long-term mission?

Build Up Your Team

The collective genius of us all is what makes us great.

When you are taking on staff you are being freed from certain tasks, but in return, you are taking on the responsibility of their welfare while at work. Building up a happy and healthy team requires intention. As the leader of your mission, you set a precedent of excellence, dedication and integrity.

A healthy operation starts at the top and trickles down into every step.

Your employees need a lot of verbal communication from you as their leader. Communication not only helps each party stay on top of any potential problems, it ensures your team feels comfortable enough to talk with you when they do. Every Monday we have a staff meeting at the Amy Howard at Home headquarters. We lovingly refer to these as our who, what, when, where, and why meetings. I verbally lay out the next week's agenda and tasks. In detail, I review who is responsible for what task, why the task is needed, where it will happen and its destination, and for when we have set the deadline. Hopefully your staff will grow to be a diverse compilation of giftings and personalities, but this also means that no two members of your staff work or communicate the same. Always refer to their DISC assessment strengths and weaknesses to help guide your communication methods. If you have a high I on staff, you will need to communicate with them differently than you do a high S.

Look for areas where you can praise and boost your team. Positivity is key to being an effective leader.

Often times as a leader, we are so excellence driven within our agenda that we can often forget to affirm our team members. It is dangerous to operate in the realm where good is never good enough. Look for areas where you can praise and boost your team. Positivity is key to being an effective leader. Everyone can always be better. Everything can always be improved upon, but without the affirmation that they are in a safe environment to grow, you will stifle their drive for such growth.

Look at your staff as extensions of your mission.

Without them, your dream can't expand. Invest in your team members' well-being. When you talk to them, use "we" instead of "I". Focus on the strengths of the people helping you accomplish the mission of your dream. Praise and acknowledge all of their hard work and successes.

Help your staff set long-term goals. If they understand how they are vital to the future, they will become invested in the present. Be honest with members about identifying potential triggers early on to later avoid larger problems. And dear maker, never lose your cool with anyone on your team. Even when problems arise or tough discussions need to take place, always stay positive. Nothing will kill morale faster than harsh and negative criticism. The team helping you accomplish the mission of your dream is your top priority.

CONSIDER THIS Just as the purpose of your mission requires focus and intent, so does the team you need to get you there. Never diminish the value of having people who believe in you enough to dedicate their time and effort to helping you get where you need to go. Right now, list out affordable monthly activities and events you can implement into your yearly calendar. These events can be as simple as a potluck party, guest speaker or sponsored local events.

The larger your company the larger your special event budget can grow. When you are starting up and only have a handful of team members, there are small thoughtful measures you can take that will still have great impact. Examples include: buying flowers for your bookkeeper's desk, surprising members with a gift card or even buying employee's lunches once a month. These seemingly trivial efforts will not only speak volumes of your appreciation, it will establish an environment of camaraderie amongst the team semblance.

YOUR EXTENDED TEAM

Every operation has an in-house team and an extended team. Initially, your extended team is generally larger than your in-house staff. Nonetheless, every member should be treated with respect and regarded as a long-term investment in your business's welfare. Vendors, suppliers, banks, logistics service companies, photographers, web designers, IT support, and attorneys are all examples of your extended team. These experts will likely see your company grow from a start-up to a full-fledged business entity. Sometimes they can even be your most trusted aids. Everyone who helps you get where you need to go is part of your team. I recommend treating them as a long-term asset.

ASK YOURSELF

Who is currently on your in-house and extended team?

What are three team-building tools or exercises you could use?

What three things could you do to make sure your team is assured they are valued?

Team Players

Growing a team comprised of different personality types and experience levels will bring its trials.

While you would hope every team member loves to work with you, that might not always be the case. When you come across a situation where an employee is not thriving or satisfied with their position, it is best to evaluate the root issues.

Miscommunication and misplaced strengths are the two main causes for an employee's indifference.

Author and speaker, Jim Collins produced a game-changing business reference entitled *Good to Great*. During his five years of research he found one overwhelming trend amongst the top eleven companies that grew from good to great. Just before their climb to the top, they turned their focus from the what to the who. Jim described his results in a bus analogy. You as the leader are driving your bus. You can go anywhere you want, but before you decide to take off, your team members must sit down. Jim explains that while you can try to point members to their appropriate seats, some of them might not belong on the bus. Some team members may not have committed themselves to your mission. If you have members who don't believe in the significance of what you are setting out to do, it's time for them to move on. In order for your bus to be ready for departure, everyone has to be on the right bus.

FIRING ANY EMPLOYEE SHOULD BE YOUR LAST RESORT. WARNINGS, HIRING A THIRD-PARTY MEDIATOR AND REARRANGING JOB DESCRIPTIONS ARE ALL IMPACTFUL TEAM-SAVING TACTICS. PUT EVERY EFFORT YOU CAN INTO GIVING AN EMPLOYEE A CHANCE TO THRIVE WITHIN YOUR MISSION. IN THE END, IF SOMEONE IS NOT A GOOD FIT, CLOSE THAT DOOR WITH GRACE AND GRATITUDE.

Likewise, you might have employees who are on the right bus, they are on board and passionate about your mission, but wrongly seated. Much like my bookkeeper, if you have a team member who has somehow slipped through the who to hire assessment and is floundering with discontent, find them a new seat. As long as everyone who is with you is, on the right bus, you can easily shuffle seats to find a better fit. It would be better to have people who believe in your mission with you than to go alone.

TOUGH CALLS

Employees who are enthusiastic about working with you within your mission are all ears when you communicate your vision and projected direction. However, there will be some members that come along who aren't so much interested in what you have to say as they are in what they have to say. You may have some employees who reveal they have their own agenda. Misguided authority is a great stumbling block in a team setting. If someone is not on your bus, it is generally because they are trying to drive their own.

Years ago, my husband Gene and I had to make one of the toughest calls in the history or our business. We had a dear employee with us for over 16 years, who worked alongside me with dedication to formulate our signature finishes. I had positioned her as a leader within our workshop. For years, she was a prized asset to our mission. During her sixteenth year, while participating in a company-wide meeting, she stood up and stated she didn't agree with our choices and wasn't going to participate. She walked out of the meeting and went back to her work in the shop. We tried coaching sessions, but in her eyes, her agenda was more important than ours.

Dear maker, when someone resists change in life, they generally don't understand their own importance in the situation.

As you will find in the DISC assessment results, when most people hear of change coming, their initial thought is, "How will this affect me?" In most cases, simply reminding them of their vital importance, no matter where you go, is enough. Remember, almost everyone is looking to be assured they are needed and important in life. Some, however, already find themselves important. So much so, they set their agenda above yours. In these instances, they would probably be better off on a different bus, as they'll never consent to being a part of yours.

The core of your mission should be visible in your workspace. Your value drivers, (i.e. excellence, creativity, and harmony) should become your team members' value drivers while they are with you. Not everyone will want to own their own business. They can have their own sense of purpose working alongside you on your bus. Get them in the right seat. Give them some authority and ownership within their position. Being on your bus can be as fulfilling for them as a participant in the journey as it is for you as the driver. Dear maker, in everything you do, uphold your mission. Growing from good to great isn't a luck of the draw. Intention, integrity, and focus in every facet of your entrepreneurial life will make your mission flourish.

ASK YOURSELF

Is everyone on your team on your bus?

In what positive ways can you ensure your team is all in and rightly seated?

Collaborating

As a mission-minded business owner, the idea of teaming up with another company can sound empowering, but also dangerous.

YOU CAN'T DO IT ALL ON YOUR OWN

Living out your mission will inspire other businesses and in time, will invite potential partnerships. Collaborating can be as simple as teaming up with another maker for a project or having a brainstorming session to bring awareness to each of your missions. Boosting each other up and promoting each other's efforts will bring your community of makership together and stronger.

Who you are collaborating with makes all the difference in the world. Your vision and their vision should clearly lineup. No matter what opportunities come your way, don't compromise on your mission statement. When you are considering forming a team, much like you do in your interviewing process, lay out a clear picture of what working together will look like. Set boundaries and expectations ahead of your projected plans. Make sure that your missions are similar either in aesthetic or agenda. Take advantage of each other's hard work by coming together for a unified effort. Your target audiences will be thankful you provided them with the benefit of growing in market awareness and consumer opportunity.

EXTEND YOUR REACH

I find that for most small business owners, the subject of partnering with a distribution platform can be a touchy subject. Often times when you have built something from the ground up, you feel it is too near and dear to your heart to let go. Distribution doesn't have to be categorized as selling out or letting go. There is nothing wrong with utilizing another company's reach to broaden your client base. This is part of their mission and they have likely worked hard to make these channels available to you.

You can team up with someone who is successful in their own process without compromising your mission or vision. Nothing has changed. Rather you are now allowing your process to be duplicated across the country. You started out as one store and one vision; when you set out to make a difference, people noticed. To further your reach and cover more ground, you must team up with someone whose mission and purpose is to help businesses like yours do just that. They have the channels in place and were established to be the bridge to your customers. The people who will help you distribute are your lifeline to your target audience. You are making up for where they lack and they are providing what you cannot provide for yourself. Think of them as part of your team.

CONSIDER THIS Why not partner with someone who can complement and support your mission? You want to make something and they want to help you get it to those people. Each of your are here for the greater purpose of providing a need in the market.

Write down three local business owners and one national brand that you would be interested in associating with in the near future. Go ahead and dream big. There are plenty of national brands who regularly partner with small local makers for events and collaborative projects. Having an ongoing list of fellow entrepreneurs that you admire enough to partner with, not only helps you set goals, it keeps your branding decisions in check.

Living out your mission will <u>inspire other businesses</u> and in time, will invite potential partnerships.

Every product you make has to have distribution. Distribution can be broken down into eight categories of benefit for you as a maker: Information, promotion, contact, client matching, price validation, transportation, financial support, and risk taking. Dear maker, you can't always be every answer; you can't always do it on your own. A good distributor will buy into your vision, your product, and your mission. They will become an extension of your team so that you are not selling out.

Over the years my business has experienced just about every facet of collaboration imaginable. From small local events to project-based team efforts, our strategy has always embraced the greatness of a collective genius. To date, one of my most impactful experiences has been the journey to team up with my boutique retailers and the Ace Hardware family. Our core value drivers are nothing short of coequal. Make sure that when you look back on any partnership or collaboration, you can say that you learned from and sharpened each other every step of the way. This is when the business of your dreams can grow into an even greater purpose.

ASK YOURSELF

What particular attributes would you like to see in a potential collaborative partner?

What three distribution channels could your business benefit from the most by teaming up with another brand?

The Road Ahead

Assess & Re-Assess

*Dear maker, this road ahead is full of adventure
and, more importantly, change.*

When you closed your eyes that day and allowed yourself to dream
again, you changed the course of your future. Every step towards growth
is a step in change. The fundamentals you gather early in this journey will
continue to guide you through growth and opportunity in the future.

Never become too comfortable or
complacent. A lack of awareness will lead
you back to idleness.

60/40

In the first days of your business, you, as the owner, will be the sole
operator for most tasks. However, as your business grows your position
should evolve as well. In the years to come, you will need to set yourself
in the role of visionary more than facilitator. I have a rule of thumb that I
spend at least sixty percent of my day building my business and no more
than forty percent running of it. Otherwise after all that dreaming and
planning, you have merely created another job for yourself.

TEAM MEMBERS

As your company grows, each team member will need a tailored strategy to focus on. Your employees should either take on more responsibilities or become more concentrated in their focus. Every time anything within a job description changes, put it in writing. Make sure as you go over the updated job description with the employee, you remind them that their contribution doesn't just stop there. One way to grow in any position is the willingness to go the extra mile when it's needed. Allow the members of your team to mature their gifts while they are working with you and then teach them to utilize those gifts as specialized skills. Each person needs to understand how their role is making sure the mission is being met and the vision is coming to pass.

POLICIES

Evaluate your operation every week, every month, and every quarter for its successes and weaknesses. Be open and honest about the necessary changes. Catch a potential trigger before it becomes a big problem. If something works, write it into a policy. It's not official until it is written down. Eventually all your team's accomplishments will derive from the duplicated processes found at the foundation of your operation.

YEARLY EMPLOYEE ASSESSMENTS ARE VITAL STRENGTH BUILDING TOOLS. EMBRACE THE OPPORTUNITY AS AN OPEN COMMUNICATION EXERCISE. AS YOU ASK QUESTIONS AND LISTEN TO ANSWERS, THEY WILL LIKELY READILY RECIPROCATE THE COURTESY.

STRESS TEST PROTECTION

While none of us knows the future, we can still plan ahead. Living like you only have today means you make the most of the present, but remain mindful of the future. Having a good strategy for the future gives your dream a leg up in the face of adversity. Examine your finances, your team members, and your policies. If any of these areas would prove weak in the midst of financial crisis or tragedy, make them stronger. To a degree, the business you are building must become self-supporting. Take the time to set your dream and your staff up for long-term and sustainable prosperity.

STOP DOING, JUST FOCUS

The mission of your dream should be your top priority. Opportunities will abound in front of you, but if a task or responsibility distracts you from your original mission, cut it out. The edit and focus rule applies to everything. Be consistent with what you have set out to accomplish. For some of you, this may mean more than cutting out social media and television, it might mean selling a property and saying no to growth opportunities. If you allow anything that doesn't align with your mission to come into your path, you allow yourself to be divided from your mission. Division will cause your business to crumble. Stay focused, dear maker.

ASK YOURSELF

What areas of your operation need the most attention?

How can you better strengthen this area to become self-sufficient?

What is distracting you? How and when can you cut it out?

Take Risks

After nearly four years of making and selling Amy Howard Collection home furnishings, I realized I had reached the limits of growth on my own.

I would have to broaden my reach to continue to grow. I wanted to have as much coverage in the United States, as simply as possible. I researched designer showrooms across the country to see who had the most locations and largest client following. I kept coming across the name Robert Allen Beacon Hill. So, I dreamed a little. What would it be like for our furniture to be in the Robert Allen Beacon Hill luxury designer showrooms throughout the country?

Without hesitation, I called Robert Allen Beacon Hill Designs' buyer in Boston, Massachusetts. I explained what set Amy Howard Collection apart. I told him how I designed the entire line of artisan hand-crafted furniture. To my astonishment, he said he would love to meet me. When he asked if I was in Boston as well, I replied, "I can be." Within days, I was boarding a plane to Boston, with a ticket I couldn't really afford, to attend a chance thirty-minute meeting. On the plane, I kept thinking "What in the world am I doing?... This is crazy!" We sat in the middle of my hotel lobby discussing our one-of-a-kind luxury designs. He looked at me and said, "We would love to have you. Lets make it happen."

CONSIDER THIS Making risky business decisions does not have to mean changing your lifestyle or business model. A risky decision can simply mean deciding to partner with a local non-profit organization or holding an open house event with other local businesses. A risk is simply participating in something that has an unforeseen outcome. More times than not, taking a risky move will often bring positive market exposure.

List out ten risky moves you can take as a business owner this year. Treat your list as a compilation of goals and yearly markers. In the immediate you can simply check off making a cold call to a local boutique that you would like to sell your products or services in. A long-term risk could involve traveling to research the international market you hope to one day emulate. Just about any business decision can be risky, so make some decisions and be a risk taker.

That bold confidence in our mission birthed an eighteen-year relationship and millions of dollars in sales. Any time I am about to make a risky decision, I get extremely nervous. I assure myself I am choosing the right path by funneling it through our mission. I always ask myself, "Does this decision uphold the integrity of my dream?"

Self trust will be your greatest ally during your journey, dear maker.

Believe in your mission so much that upholding it becomes a conviction. Doing so will give you the drive to become bold in your choices. You must feel so strongly about your purpose that you are willing to do what it takes to see it grow. For me, I go back to the beginning. Remember that moment when I knew this is what I was supposed to be doing. Know that fear will always come in. Anchor yourself to your moment. It will give you the strength to keep going forward.

Believe in your mission so much that upholding it becomes a conviction.

Dear maker, if one of your ideas flops, this doesn't mean the whole production is a sham. As you step out in risk, you test the waters. Build on your successes and learn from the failures. Just as you celebrate your successes, understand those failures. Why did it fail? What were the steps that caused the results to fall short? Repeat your assessment process. Weed out the choices that didn't end in success and write the successful choices into a company policy. If you fail to step out and take a risk, you may never know what you are missing.

ASK YOURSELF

What bold moves have you already made in this adventure?

What are three risky moves you are contemplating right now?

What will succeeding in those risks do for the business of your purpose and your mission?

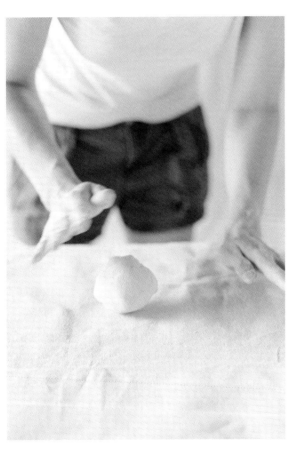

Roll with the Punches

Come 2011, after nearly twenty years of making furniture, my target audience completely changed.

We began to see that ninety percent of the furniture sold in the United States was being made overseas. Designers who had been in business for over twenty years were closing their doors and many were deciding to retire. Even their wealthiest clients no longer had a decorating budget. The purchasing of furniture became primarily price-driven, paying no mind to quality. I began to see copies of our original designs sold for less than half the price. It was heart wrenching, to say the least.

Our competition was knocking off my art. I would draw every design by hand. After each piece was cut, I would hold it up and see if it was exactly how I imagined. Every design had to feel right. Now my hard work was being copied and made overseas by people who had no ownership in the design. It was a devastating loss.

If we were going to stay in business, I had to think outside the box. There had to be a change in how we diversified the brand. Our customer was no longer the luxury buyer, but rather the twenty-three year old DIY blogger and the sixty-five year old retiree taking up a woodworking hobby. While there was some connection to the Amy Howard Collection, our mission was a lot larger and our demographic was much broader. We were now responsible for teaching and inspiring our customers, not just supplying them with furniture.

EVERY 2, 5, 10 AND 20 YEARS YOUR COMPETITIVE MARKET WILL EXPERIENCE A MASSIVE BELL CURVE. IT HAS NOTHING TO DO WITH YOUR DREAM, IT IS JUST THE WAY THE MARKET IS WIRED TO GROW. IN ANY SCENARIO, THAT BELL CURVE IS A CHANCE TO EITHER RIDE YOUR CURRENT MISSION THROUGH OR BUILD YOUR MOMENTUM INTO A WHOLE NEW ADVENTURE.

Every new business idea must be a solution
to a problem.

Dreams change as we develop personally. Many times your existing business evolves to a point where a brand new idea can be a birthed. I like to refer to this as your bell curve. Over the course of your business, your sales are going to reach a peak and then possibly have a downward slope. That doesn't mean you have failed. This is just the cycle of business. When you're at the top of that bell curve, when the business is doing well, you need to look at where you are going next. Dear maker, always be thinking about ways to diversify and build on your existing dream.

ASK YOURSELF

How will you know when you're at the top of your bell curve?

What ideas do you have for the future of you company?

If you could grow in any area of your hedgehog where would it be?

Our Blue Ocean Strategy

*Dear maker, that same competitive market you set
out to conquer can also drain you.*

When the landscape grows so aggressive that you begin to lose the
joy of your mission, it is time to look at another venue. Your next phase
should be an extension of your original dream and compliment your
prior mission. Everything you have been working for up to this point,
every choice you have made, should lead you right here.

Authors and professors Renee Mauborgne and W. Chan Kim co-
wrote *Blue Ocean Strategy* about just this problem. This decade-long
study spans thirty industries, revealing principles to empower every
business owner to find uncontested market space. Their data taught me
how to bring my mission to the market at a lower cost, while staying true
to my value drivers, profit margin, and target audience. It was time to
focus on what we could offer that wouldn't just outperform, it would be
incontestable. It all came back to our hedgehog.

I dug deep into my core and asked myself, "What do we do better
than anyone else?" One noteworthy attribute spanned the course of
our time as entrepreneurs. From our past, restoring rescues, to our
present, designing and building furniture, our finishes set Amy Howard
Collection pieces apart. From studying in a Bodega and scouring the
Paris flea market to working in our own home and stores, our passion
for developing and experimenting with our products revealed an even
greater purpose. The Amy Howard at Home paint line was born. As an
art history major, I not only studied what made an antique look antiqued,
but engineered a one-of-a-kind replication process. My skills had
become so seasoned it felt natural to teach on the subject.

CONSIDER THIS Your "blue ocean strategy" isn't something you can accomplish in the early days of your business, rather it emerges when you are seasoned, trained, and structured enough to gain that unmatched standing. This is where all of your focus, discipline, and intentional choices prove worthy to be set apart as a voice of authority. Remember we discussed how roughly 10,000 hours is needed to gain mastery in a field? Your blue ocean strategy is the business of that mastery.

Based on what you are working towards, in this stage of your business, what do you believe you have the potential to master? This is where you need to focus the majority of your attention. Write this long-term goal into your business plan. Staying focused on your blue ocean strategy won't be easy when faced with a sea of opportunities, but like everything else, seeing it in writing will keep you accountable in the years to come.

Our products were set apart because they were not only artisan inspired, but they came with the expert's secrets. I saw our chalk-based paint as the tool for showing people how they could create their own artistic pieces. Unlike any other chalk based paint, ours could be used without any waxes or finishers. Our lacquers are professional grade and our venetian plaster is made with real marble. No other line provides the DIY hobbyist this same level of quality.

While at dinner with Mike and Debbi Rose of Mrs. Fields Cookies, we decided the name of the line should be Amy Howard At Home. We already had the brand name Amy Howard Collection and it was important to respect the following we had built up for twenty-one years. Our tagline words validated the mission of our brand. "Rescue, restore, redecorate" embodied our new dream. We were already known for making beautiful handcrafted furniture. Now we were sharing our processes and procedures, teaching others how to create those same finishes and turn it into a business of their own.

THE ROAD AHEAD | 169

That hedgehog of finishes became our "blue ocean strategy." We were ready to go out into those uncharted waters and no longer be shoulder to shoulder with everyone copying each other. We were not just artisan and handmade, we were in a league of our own.

ASK YOURSELF

Do you have any idea what your "blue ocean strategy" would be?

How does it fit into your current mission?

Conclusion

———

Dear Maker,

You have come so far and grown by leaps and bounds in this short amount of time.

Even now, though there is hard work to be done and tough decisions to be made, your future holds so much more promise than before. Leading a disciplined life, one that chases after excellence, is far more fulfilling than existing only in circumstance. I encourage you to find strength in the belief that you are making a difference in people's lives. As long as your efforts as a creative entrepreneur are honorable and needed, they are important.

Even though some days you will wake up exhausted, you have to be willing to continually pursue this mission you set out to accomplish. Never be happy with status quo, but ever willing to refine your hedgehog. Know that there is so much more to learn. Read books dear maker, lots and lots of books. I have gained as much knowledge, if not more, from my daily business reading than I did while earning my business degree. Find a mentor to learn from. Those who have walked before you have invaluable advice, wisdom and foresight. Having a guide to lead you through these early days is what, I believe, will make your journey all the more successful.

Every word I have placed inside this book, I use everyday. I have written to you, because I want to see you succeed; to have the satisfaction of working hard and seeing that work reap reward. You have not started your business to see it fail. No matter how big or how small your business is, you must constantly refine the foundation it is built on. I want to give you the tools you need to see your business grow and thrive. You don't have to set out to own a million-dollar operation, you just have to make sure you are doing what you love, with excellence.

As you not only work hard, but also work smart, you will find every year will bring growth, opportunity and prosperity to your business. Utilize this book as an ongoing roadmap and reference. There will be unforeseen events that arise, but the basics found within these pages are applicable throughout every stage. I encourage you to stay true to your calling as a creative entrepreneur by never allowing yourself to forget the immeasurable value you have found in utilizing the gifts that are specific only to you. You are needed dear maker. This world needs what you hold.

Sources

86% MILLIONAIRES, *as referenced in Gifting + Passion = Purpose*
In depth survey conducted by Fidelity Investments analyzing more than 1,000 millionaire households, Fidelity Millionaire Outlook, Fidelity Investments Institutional Services Company, Inc. (2012, FMR LLC.)

DISC PERSONALITY TYPES, *as referenced in Who You Are*
Discpersonalitytesting.com, (2015, Guy Harris and Kevin Eikenberry)

10,000 HOURS TO MASTERY, *as referenced in Committed*
Study of alternative tactics to understand success and make the most of our human potential, *Outliers*, Malcolm Gladwell, (2008, Little, Brown and Company)

SOCIAL MEDIA, *as referenced in Where Are You Falling Short?*
Data gathered from 2010 to 2014 on the average daily media use in the United States, statistica.com (Statistica Inc.)

HEDGEHOG & ON THE BUS, *as referenced in Competitive Landscape*
Study of 11 companies that made substantial improvements in their performance over time, *Good to Great*, Jim Collins (2001, HarperBusiness)

BLUE OCEAN STRATEGY, *as referenced in Our Blue Ocean Strategy*
Study of 150 strategic business moves that create a leap in value within an uncontested market share, *Blue Ocean Strategy*, W. Chan Kim and Renee Mauborgne (2005, Harvard Business School Press)

Thank You

────

While writing a book for makers has been a dream of mine for quite some time, I knew that in order for it to be everything I envisioned, I needed a team. A writer to bring my words to life, a designer to create graceful visual pauses and a photographer to capture the essence of my messages. But to simply partner with other creative people wouldn't be enough. I needed my dream to become their dream – I needed kindred spirits.

God gave an opportunity for the dream of writing to be birthed in Tarra Kruzan. Countless hours of stories and instruction were shared – sometimes with laughter and others with tears. She truly dreamed with me as we wrote and rewrote the roadmap of A Maker's Guide. I fell in love with her spirit and desire to do everything with excellence!

Candace Joseph is a gifted graphic design artist whose eye for detail, composition and ability to serve as art director has truly been a gift. She took thousands of words and images and brought them to a cohesive visual masterpiece. Her drive, professionalism and ever-willing heart constantly inspires me.

Annabella Charles is an award winning photographer that sees the world in picture form. Her infectious love for life and those around her is displayed in every image she captures. Her attention to detail and a deep connection to her projects has made it a sheer delight to work together.

The collaboration I have experienced with these incredibly gifted women, has been nothing short of a miraculous provision from heaven. Working with world class people, who know their gifts and are willing to focus on one goal, can be life changing. I know it was for me. Thank you Tarra, Candace and Annabella for being three amazing women whom I have grown to love. I take pride in being your maker mom.

I want to thank my children Brooke, Megan, Preston and Stephanie for allowing me to be me, for loving me in spite of my failures and for being the most creative, intelligent, hard-working entrepreneurs I know. Your passions encourage me more than you could ever realize.

To my parents, Myron and Ruby Coney, thank you for instilling the spirit of business in me, for teaching me to work hard – to never give up and for giving me a great legacy by loving each other for 71 years.

To the Amy Howard at Home team of creatives. Your dedication, love for our mission and belief in the greater good of my dream has driven me to accomplish more than I ever believed possible. I am honored to be on this journey together.

To Debbi Fields, my mentor, friend and confidant. You inspire me, believe in me and have selflessly given of yourself in ways only a loyal friend would. Thank you from the bottom of my heart for walking this road with me.

And to my husband Gene, who possesses a truly unconditional love for me. You have allowed me the freedom to dream big and what's more, you have dreamed right beside me. Your support and friendship is a soft place for me to land at the end of a trying day. You remind me to keep my poker face in the Paris flea markets and you carry boxes of antique books on the plane with a smile. You rub my feet when I am tired and tell me I'm beautiful when my mascara is smudged from crying. Most of us desire to have just one person in our lives that believes the best in us. For me, you have always been that person. I thank God for giving me the gift of you.

Creative beings are born with distinguishable aptness and the inventive ability to think outside the box. The capability to turn such talents and ideas into a sustainable income however, can quickly become a pitfall.

A MAKER'S GUIDE is a comprehensive roadmap written to those who desire to start a business using the giftings that have been a part of their makeup since childhood. Touching on every stage of the entrepreneurial journey – from paralyzing fear to creating incontestable strategies – author Amy Howard, founder of Artisan Studios, Amy Howard Collection and Amy Howard at Home, counsels artistic minds with her personal and business expertise collected from her own 30 year venture. Howard's curated letter is comprised of pragmatic business instruction, the discipline of intention and a petition to pursue the freedom and satisfaction found only in following a dream.

———

AMY HOWARD, owner of the Amy Howard at Home lifestyle line, has continually refined her affinities for timeless artisanship her entire life. At the beginning of 1991, Amy and Gene Howard launched their luxury furniture business, Amy Howard Collection. With their one-of-a-kind refinished vintage rescues and handmade couture furnishings, the Amy Howard name was set apart as an authority in interior design. Come 2012, after three decades of making luxurious home furnishings, Amy and Gene utilized their curated expertise to create a fully encompassed line of professional grade artisan products. The mission to rescue, restore and redecorate has since brought hope to like-minded creatives by teaching the weekend hobbyist how to become a self-supporting business owner. Her experience as a successful entrepreneur and her willingness to share her lifetime of knowledge, has brought her career to an inspiring crescendo. Today, Amy Howard is partnering with the artisan community on a journey to craft a beautiful life and build a legacy.